SWEET CHILD

BORN IN

CALIFORNIA

CALIFORNIA REPUBLIC

Whitney Strauss
with Susan Giles and
Dr. Kathleen Cooter, PhD

Illustrated by
Cynthia Meadows

KIDS

BROWN BOOKS KIDS

Sweet Child Born in California

Brown Books Kids
Dallas, TX / New York, NY
www.BrownBooksKids.com
(972) 381-0009

A New Era in Publishing®

Publisher's Cataloging-In-Publication Data

Names: Strauss, Whitney, author. | Giles, Susan, author. | Cooter, Kathleen Spencer, 1950- author. | Meadows, Cynthia, illustrator.
Title: Sweet child born in California / Whitney Strauss, with Susan Giles and Dr. Kathleen Cooter, PhD ; illustrated by Cynthia Meadows.
Description: Dallas, Texas : Brown Books Kids, [2020] | Series: [Sweet child United States] ; [2] | Interest age level: 003-008. | Summary: "Sweet Child Born in California is the second book in the educational series that is teaching kids across the country about their home states--and teaching others what makes each state worth a visit! Packed with state facts and history, this book beams with pride for the Golden State"--Provided by publisher.
Identifiers: ISBN 9781612544243
Subjects: LCSH: California--Description and travel--Juvenile literature. | California--History--Juvenile literature. | Emblems, State--California--Juvenile literature. | CYAC: California--Description and travel. | California--History. | Emblems, State--California. | LCGFT: Stories in rhyme.
Classification: LCC F861.3 .S77 2020 | DDC 917.94 979.4 [E]--dc23

ISBN 978-1-61254-424-3
LCCN 2019909857

Printed in the United States
10 9 8 7 6 5 4 3 2 1

For more information or to contact the authors, please go to
www.SweetChildSeries.com.

DEDICATION

This book is dedicated to our children, who have enriched our lives with their love, laughter, and curiosity. Being your moms has been the blessing of our lives.

ACKNOWLEDGMENTS

So much love and gratitude to Rob, Randy, and Bob for their continued support. Special thank you to Brown Books for believing in us and cheering us on to continue to write these special books.

Welcome to California, sweet child,
nicknamed the Golden State.
There are such wondrous things
that make our California great!

California is a BIG state
with lots of room to play.
It is the third-largest state
in the entire USA.

Sacramento

San Francisco

San Jose

HOLLYWOOD

Los Angeles

Long Beach

San Diego

Sacramento is the capital;
Los Angeles, the largest city.
Travel to San Jose, San Francisco,
San Diego, or Long Beach—they're all so pretty!

The state bird is the quail;
the state insect's the dogface butterfly.
Our state mammal is the grizzly bear,
and golden trout swim in streams nearby.

The state flower is the California poppy;
coast redwood is the state tree.

Gold is the state mineral.
Such stunning things we see!

and on to the towering
redwood forests
where trees can live a
thousand years.

Sourdough is the state bread;
many fruits and vegetables grow here—
avocados, grapes, strawberries, and lettuce.
Enjoy it all, my dear!

Presidents Hoover, Nixon, and Reagan
have called California their home.

Palo Alto

Santa Barbara

San Clemente

Disneyland and Hollywood
are places children and movie stars roam.

So, sweet child born in California,
feel such pride in what you see.
"Eureka! I found it!" is the motto here;
a Californian is what you are meant to be!

ABOUT THE AUTHORS: THE SWEET MAMAS

WHITNEY STRAUSS is the busy working mom of two boys and an active volunteer in a variety of children's charities in Dallas. She and her husband, Rob, enjoy visiting the California coast as often as possible.

SUSAN GILES is not only a busy working mom but also the very active grandma of six grandsons. She has traveled the country in her career and hopes that the Sweet Child United States series will help children appreciate each state's distinct treasures. She and her husband, Randy, love their native state of Tennessee, and she wants to share the story of the Volunteer State soon as well!

KATHLEEN COOTER is a retired university professor of early education who currently lives in Texas. She is a mom to three adult kids and has many beloved grandchildren. It is her hope that families read and share this book and that it becomes a treasured keepsake.

ABOUT THE ILLUSTRATOR

CYNTHIA MEADOWS, a native Texan, was first inspired in her art by Winnie the Pooh and *The Wind in the Willows*. She hopes her own illustrations inspire the imaginations of children with a similar love of books.